Restaurant Marketing Magic

How to Boost Your Restaurant's
Profits by 30% or More with the
#1 Dining Holiday

Sean Payne

For related information and materials, please visit our website at www.BirthdayMarketing.us

Between the time website information is gathered and then published, it is not unusual for some websites to have closed or changed. Also, transcription of URLs may contain typographical errors. If you spot any, please notify the publisher so they can be corrected in subsequent editions.

ISBN-13: 978-1523687602

ISBN-10: 1523687606

Disclaimer:

This book is for information purposes only. It does not in any way, shape, or form provide legal or financial advice. I can't and won't promise that you'll make money by using the information in this book, because only you can control whether you actually implement it or not.. Read it, learn from it, and decide for yourself whether it's a good idea for you to implement it in your own business.

Table of Contents

Introduction

Are you looking for ways to generate more business for your restaurant?

Want to attract new customers and generate positive cash flow from a unique source you probably aren't using yet?

Would you like to get more foot traffic, increase sales, and improve customer retention?

If so, this guide is the answer you're looking for. It will introduce you to my secret system for bringing in new business and getting the exposure your restaurant needs.

Businesses as large as Disney are using this method to increase their revenues, even in this down economy. And businesses as small as Mom & Pop diners are using the same method to grow their business.

And, once you know the secret, you can start applying it to grow your own business.

The Secret Source for Customers

Did you know that by taking advantage of the world's #1 dining holiday, you have a virtually limitless source of new customers who will spend more and bring their friends with them?

Even better, these folks are always in a good mood, and there's little (if any) competition from other restaurants on this holiday.

Best of all, once you bring them in *once* on this holiday, they're your customers for life!

So what is this secret source for customers? What is the world's #1 dining holiday?

If you haven't guessed already, it's <u>birthdays</u>!

It's true: everybody has a birthday, and most people celebrate their birthday with some kind of special meal. They love to bring their friends with them, and they nearly always spend more than usual.

Read on to find out how you can take advantage of this "secret source" to grow your restaurant.

What is Birthday Marketing?

Birthday Marketing means offering special promotions to people on or around their birthday to entice them to go to your business.

Most restaurant owners say that the top three challenges they face are:

1) Keeping your restaurant full during non-peak hours
2) Building your own loyal tribe of repeat customers in this economy
3) Breaking through the clutter and getting customers to respond to your advertising and marketing messages

Keep reading to see how Birthday Marketing solves all three of these challenges.

What is a Birthday Club?

In addition to talking about Birthday Marketing, we're going to discuss Birthday Clubs. So, what is a Birthday Club?

A Birthday Club is also known as a "VIP Club" or a "frequent diner's club", and is basically an in-house list that you can use to send offers to people who've already visited your restaurant. It's a great way to build your own tribe of loyal customers, which is especially important in today's economy.

While Birthday Marketing is a good way to bring in <u>new</u> customers, a Birthday Club is a good way to <u>keep</u> customers once you've brought them in.

As you might guess, a Birthday Club goes hand-in-hand with Birthday Marketing, and each amplifies the power of the other.

The goal of Birthday Marketing should always be to get people to join your Birthday Club. This gives you a profitable long-term asset in the form of your Birthday Club customer database.

Why Should You Use Birthday Marketing?

The simple reason to use Birthday Marketing is because it works. Later on, I'll show you some case studies of businesses that have used Birthday Marketing to boost their business.

Below are some additional details on why Birthday Marketing works, and how implementing Birthday Marketing for your restaurant can increase your revenues significantly.

Birthday Popularity

Birthdays are the #1 occasion for celebrating with a special meal. In fact, more than 55% of Americans dine out on their birthday, far more than the next-most popular holidays (Valentine's Day and Mother's Day). In addition, around 70% of adults will visit a restaurant on their own birthday or someone else's birthday.

People love to get birthday gifts, and they love the businesses that give those gifts to them. They will remember those birthday gifts year after year, and it makes them want to come back to your restaurant throughout the year.

Create Goodwill

Birthdays make people happy, and those happy people tend to spend more (nearly $80 per table, on average), have a better time, and tip better. So, not only are birthdays good for your restaurant's bottom line, they're good for your wait staff, too!

And, since people rarely dine alone on their birthdays, you'll get larger groups. The average birthday table is 3.75 people. Even better, around 30% of those people will be at your restaurant for the first time. Just imagine what it will mean to your bottom line if they become repeat customers!

Generate More Business from Existing Customers

A great birthday offer is an easy way to get your existing customers to come back to your restaurant for their birthday. In fact, over 28% of people said they are extremely likely to spend their birthday at their favorite restaurant if it has a birthday or frequent diners club. So, in addition to all the other times they eat at your restaurant, they'll spend one of the most profitable holidays with you as well.

A special birthday gift also helps to give you top-of-mind presence with your customers, so you're the first place they think of when they want to dine out.

Create Word-of-Mouth Buzz about Your Restaurant

Can you imagine being the restaurant that everyone talks about? Birthday Marketing is a great way to create a groundswell of satisfied customers who will tell everyone they know about the great birthday gift they got from your restaurant.

After all, everybody wants to be the one "in the know" who can share something special with their friends. Birthday Marketing positions your restaurant to be the special thing that they want to share.

Bring in New Customers

In addition to getting your existing customers to come back more often, an attractive birthday offer is also an excellent way to get new guests in the front door. Through using some creative methods (which we'll discuss later), you can get your birthday offer out to people who've never dined with you before, and have the chance to convert them to regular customers.

Increased Profitability

As you can see, Birthday Marketing has the potential to improve short-term profitability by bringing in larger groups, encouraging more frequent visits by existing customers, and taking advantage of increased birthday spending patterns. Even better, it can also result in higher long-term profitability by bringing in new customers and then turning them into repeat customers.

Just to give you an idea of how Birthday Marketing can lead to increased profitability, the National Restaurant Association estimates that if you include all of the above increased profitability factors, <u>the value of an average birthday dinner table is $2,500 over a five-year period</u>. Definitely something to keep in mind as you put together your own Birthday Marketing plan.

Summary

As you can see, Birthday Marketing has incredible potential to bring in new customers, get regular customers to come back more often and spend more, increase foot traffic, improve sales and customer retention, and boost your overall profitability.

How can you afford not to start using Birthday Marketing?

Interesting Birthday Marketing Statistics

55%
dine out on their birthday

Birthdays are the most popular occasion to dine out

Percentage of adults who visit a restaurant on their own or somebody else's birthday

70%

30%

Percentage of birthday dinner guests who are at that restaurant for the first time

Average number of guests at a birthday table

3.75

$78

Average total ticket at a birthday meal table

Average value of a birthday marketing table over 5 years

$2500

10-15%

Percentage of independent restaurants that have any kind of birthday club

Birthday Marketing Case Studies

Here are just a few case studies of businesses that have used their own Birthday Marketing strategies to increase sales and profitability. These may help give you some ideas for how you can implement Birthday Marketing for your own restaurant.

Boneheads Restaurant

Boneheads Restaurant created a Birthday Club and used online Birthday Marketing to promote their birthday offer to new and existing customers.

After 30 days, here are the results they got:

- # of new Facebook fans: 29
- # of people who filled out their online Birthday Club form: 86
- # of people who redeemed a birthday offer coupon: 51
- Average ticket: $78.21
- Total revenue generated: $3,988.71

It should also be noted that 30% of the people who came were first-time visitors to Boneheads Restaurant.

If their results are consistent over the next 12 months, Boneheads Restaurant will see the following results:

- 350-450 new Facebook fans
- 1,032 email addresses added to their database
- 612 birthday offer coupon redemptions
- $48,529.30 in additional revenue generated by Birthday Marketing

This does not even factor in repeat visits from new guests during that year, which could be significant. Obviously, their Birthday Marketing strategy is a success for Boneheads Restaurant.

Brasilia Churrasco Steakhouse

This restaurant created a Birthday Club and used online Birthday Marketing to promote their offer to local residents. With a modest advertising budget, here are the results they saw within the first 25 days:

- # of people who filled out their online Birthday Club signup form: 157
- # of people who redeemed a birthday offer coupon: 93
- They continue to see between 3 and 5 online Birthday Marketing forms filled out every day.

As with Boneheads Restaurant, roughly 30% of Birthday Marketing guests are dining for their first time at Brasilia Churrasco Steakhouse.

Kelly O'Bryan's Neighborhood Restaurant

This restaurant chain was the very first to introduce their "Birthday Tradition" (eat free on your birthday). For over twenty-six years, Kelly O'Bryan's has offered a completely free birthday meal with just a few rules:

1) Come in on the day of your birthday
2) Bring at least one friend
3) You can spell your name correctly
4) You can prove it's your birthday

Since they started their Birthday Tradition, Kelly O'Bryan's has given over 300,000 free meals to birthday boys and girls.

As you can see by the rules above, the restaurant has a guarantee that each free birthday meal will be accompanied by at least one paid meal, and often two or more paid meals.

This effective Birthday Marketing strategy has made Kelly O'Bryan's the birthday destination for people who live near one of their multiple locations.

And, although specific figures are not available from the restaurant chain, the fact that they have continued this tradition for over twenty-six years and over 300,000 meals is strong evidence that it works well for them.

Disney World

Not even America's #1 family destination was immune to the economic downturn of 2008. Their response? Disney started actively marketing their birthday program and gave a FREE park pass to everyone on their birthday.

Many business owners worry giving away something of value for free, and don't focus on their long-term return on investment (ROI).

As Disney World's experience shows, when you give something of value to someone on their birthday, they will want to share that experience with their friends and family.

In Disney's case, a free birthday pass typically resulted in a family of four coming to the park. One person received a free pass while the other three paid to enter.

So, instead of missing out on 100% of the revenue from that family, who wouldn't have come on their own, they now had three paying guests. Even better, many of them paid extra to add additional days to their visit.

Here's a great reason why Disney's Birthday Marketing strategy can work well for your restaurant:

Disney loses money when guests don't come to their park, because their overhead expenses alone are astronomical. They're paying for staff, maintenance, electricity, and so on, regardless of how many people are walking through the front gate.

So, instead of continuing to lose money by leaving the park empty, they give a gift (free birthday passes) to get people in the door, knowing that they will bring friends and family with them. It's no wonder they're seeing increased profits year after year.

In the same way, your overhead expenses when your restaurant is empty in the middle of the week can eat away at your profits. Instead of just letting your restaurant sit empty, be bold and use Disney World's strategy of giving a free gift to get people in the front door. You may just increase your profits like Disney did.

How to Do Your Own Birthday Marketing

A good Birthday Marketing strategy has many moving parts and will require a fair amount of effort and organization to get it started, but it can provide a substantial return on investment compared to other forms of advertising.

The step-by-step checklist below will show you how to start doing your own Birthday Marketing using postcard mailings.

Also, make sure to check out the later section on how to boost your Birthday Marketing results by using email, text messaging, and online advertising.

> If you don't want the trouble of doing your own Birthday Marketing, you can go to www.BirthdayMarketing.us/postcard-dfy to see our done-for-you postcard Birthday Marketing service. It's a great time saver, and you'll get the same great results.

Step 1: Craft Your Birthday Offer

As you may have noticed from the Case Studies above, your birthday gift, or "offer", is the key to getting results from your Birthday Marketing. A well-crafted offer will get you good results. Conversely, a poorly-crafted offer will get you poor results.

Here are some important things to keep in mind when crafting your birthday offer:

- <u>Offer something valuable</u> – nothing says "We recognize and appreciate you as a customer" like something free. It can be a free dessert, a free appetizer, a free entrée, or even a free meal. The more valuable, the more memorable it will be and the better response rates you'll get.

  Don't go cheap and offer just a measly 20% discount...it makes you look bad and leaves a bad taste in the customer's mouth. Give generously, and you will succeed. As you may have noticed, Kelly O'Bryan's has given away 300,000 meals, and it has worked well for them.

- <u>Few if any restrictions</u> – Don't devalue your gift by making your guest jump through a bunch of hoops to use it. Most people will bring one or more guests (the average birthday table is 3.75 people), so the easier you make it for your guests to redeem your offer, the more likely they'll come in.

- <u>Make it expire</u> – The only restriction that usually helps, rather than hurts, your response rate is limiting how long the offer is valid. For example, if you only accept redemptions during the week or month of their birthday.

A limited-time offer increases the perceived value of your offer, because it's not always going to be available. This means they have to take advantage of it *now*, before it goes away. It also limits the redemption period so you can track response rates to specific mailings or promotions.

Step 2: Design Your Advertising

This step assumes that you will be using a mailed offer. If you are using online / electronic methods to send out your offer, adapt the instructions below to suit the advertising method you use.

- Use postcards, not envelopes – Postcards are easier to print, address, and mail than cards or letters in envelopes. They're also cheaper to mail, and come in a variety of sizes from standard postcard size (6" x 4.25") up to a gigantic 8.5" x 11". Keep in mind that postcards over 6" x 4.25" will require more postage, and anything over 11.5" x 6.125" will be charged the "large envelope" or "flat" rate (most expensive).

- Work with a professional designer – A poorly-designed card makes you look bad and will have poor response rates. Spend some money up front to have a professional graphic designer create an attractive, colorful, eye-catching design for your postcard. A good postcard design will likely cost you $200-300.

Make sure the graphic designer you work with has direct-response marketing experience, or they will miss some key ingredients that will help your postcard get the biggest possible response.

- Showcase your offer on the front side – this is where you'll include your headline, greeting, recipient's name (if possible), your restaurant's logo / name, the birthday offer, and any fine print (e.g. "Cannot be used with other discounts").

- Address and postage on the back – the United States Postal Service has specific requirements for how much space should be left for postage and addressing, so *make sure to work with a graphic designer who is familiar with these requirements, or your postcard mailings may be rejected by the* _post office_. Our done-for-you postcard designs will meet all USPS requirements.

The addressed back side will be face-up in the mailbox, so make sure the design on this side also indicates that this is a birthday card with a worthwhile offer on the front side, to avoid having your card trash-canned.

- Help them find you – make sure your guests can find your restaurant by including a map on the back of the card. Also make sure to list your address, website, and phone number on the back of the card.

Go to www.BirthdayMarketing.us/postcards for done-for-you postcard designs, printing, and mailing services at affordable prices.

<u>Step 3: Collect and Store Information</u>

Once you've designed your mailings, you need to set up a system for collecting guests' birthday information and storing it in an electronic database.

- **Create signup forms** – these don't have to be fancy, but they do need to capture the information listed below.
    1. Name
    2. Address
    3. City, State, ZIP
    4. Phone
    5. Email
    6. Birthday date
    7. Anniversary date
    8. Email disclaimer & opt-in / opt-out

    More information is better, and it will be easier to get if you're offering a <u>great</u> birthday gift (e.g. a free meal).

Go to www.BirthdayMarketing.us for beautiful sign-up forms customized for your restaurant.

- **Set up your database system** – this can be as simple as a Microsoft Excel spreadsheet, or it can be as robust and flexible as a "real" database or Customer Relationship Manager (CRM) program.

  Whichever you choose, make sure you know how to use it and that it has the functionality that you need. You can also choose to start off in Microsoft Excel and later import your data into a true database.

  Make sure that your files are backed up regularly and stored off-site or "in the cloud". You don't want your hard-earned Birthday Club database to vanish permanently if your computer breaks or a virus corrupts your files.

- **Plan your signup strategies** – You can use one or many Birthday Marketing methods to get people to join your Birthday Club. Look at the list below and see which method(s) will work best for you:

1. <u>Mail postcards to a targeted list</u> – if you want to get your Birthday Club started quickly, you can purchase a targeted mailing list of all residents near your restaurant who have birthdays in a specific month.

   There are many list brokers available, so make sure to choose one that will allow you to select the exact geographic area you want, and narrow the list to match the demographics of your ideal customer, including birth month.

   A "cold list" of names for a birthday month can cost around $0.20 per name or less, depending on the demographics you select and the number of names you buy at once.

Once you've purchased your targeted mailing list, it's just a matter of addressing, stamping, and mailing your postcards to the names on that targeted list.

See which list broker we recommend, and get your targeted list at 10% off by going to www.BirthdayMarketing.us/list-broker

2. <u>Birthday Club signup cards</u> – these are handed out and collected by servers. Make sure that there are enough cards for everyone at the table. Hand them out (with pens) while people are waiting for appetizers – it gives them something to do while they wait.

3. <u>Feedback cards</u> – your comment cards can double as Birthday Club signup cards if you put a form on the back of the card.

4. <u>Online signup form</u> – give your customers the option of signing up for your Birthday Club on your website.

Make sure the signup form is on the top of the page or a link is prominently displayed on your website. Put a similar signup form on your restaurant's Facebook fan page.

5. <u>Fishbowl</u> – have Birthday Club signup forms, pen, and a container for completed forms in high-traffic parts of your restaurant (e.g. near the entrance) so guests can sign up for the Birthday Club.

- **Use interior advertising** – Make sure that your Birthday Club is advertised inside your restaurant. Eye-catching posters, table tents, and menu inserts can entice your guests to sign up for your Birthday Club.

> Save time and money on your interior advertising materials.
> We have customized done-for-you materials at www.BirthdayMarketing.us

- **Database entry** — Develop a system for taking completed Birthday Club signup forms and entering them into your database. Schedule this into the daily routine, and make only one person responsible for doing this. Why one person? Because if more than one person is responsible, nobody's going to do it.

  If any of the signup forms is for a birthday in the next month and that month's mailing has already gone out, have a stack of birthday offer cards available so you can address and send them one immediately.

Step 4: Offer Redemption

When your guests come in, you need to have a system already in place for them to redeem their birthday gift. Take the time in advance to carefully set up this system so there will be no snags when guests come.

Your "birthday procedure" must be the same every time, and everyone on your staff must know exactly what is supposed to happen, and who is supposed to do it. And, most of all, it has to be impressive and memorable for your guests.

- **Point of Sale System** – add a "birthday offer" discount to your Point of Sale system so you can track how many birthday offers were redeemed, and the total amount of the discounts.

  Make sure to check with your local / state sales tax codes to see whether the sales tax percentage should be applied to the actual amount paid, or to the undiscounted / retail value of the guests' bills.

- **Get your staff onboard** – make sure that all staff members understand how to handle redemptions. A great birthday offer can turn sour if it is mishandled by your staff. Hold a brief training and create an informational memo that covers the following points:

o Goals of the Birthday Club, and why it's important that it succeeds (make sure to mention *higher tips* for your staff)
o What the birthday offer includes, and what it doesn't include (which menu items, and what discounts apply)
o Restrictions on the offer (e.g. "must bring a friend")
o How to ring up the sale in the POS and apply the offer discount
o How to promote the Birthday Club to guests
o How birthday guests are to be welcomed and treated (e.g. birthday song, balloons, etc.)

• **Record Results** – make recording your redemption results part of the daily routine. Have a specific place where servers and cashiers put all birthday offer redemptions, either as they come in or at end of shift.

Appoint a single person (i.e. manager) to record all redemptions in a tracking spreadsheet. Make sure to include the number of people in each group, the total check, and the value of the free gift. Most of all, be consistent about recording your results, and you'll be sure to get ever-better results over time.

Step 5: Kick Off Your Mailings

The long-term success of your Birthday Marketing postcard mailings depends on doing them consistently and tracking results.

- **Set a Regular Mailing Date** – If you are doing physical postcard mailings, your birthday offer should be valid for the entire month of their birthday. Make sure to mail a week before the start of the month to allow time for the postcard to be delivered before the first birthday of the month.

- **Schedule Staff** – If you will be having your staff handle addressing and stamping the birthday offer postcards, make sure to schedule enough staff and processing time so your cards will go out as scheduled. This is a good task for down times and slow days.

- **Make it look hand-addressed** – Printed address labels are okay, but you will likely get better redemption rates if you address the postcards by hand. Alternatively, you can have the addresses printed in a font that looks hand-written. Also, a hand-applied postage stamp (slightly crooked, so it looks like it was done by hand) gives the postcard a personal touch.

- **Track your mailings** – Use the Promotion Tracking Worksheet (see link below) to keep track of how many total postcards went out, including how many went to each ZIP code or neighborhood. You can use this information to see which ZIP codes or neighborhoods give you the best response rates and make the most money for you.

> Download your own free copy of our Promotion Tracking Worksheet by going to www.BirthdayMarketing.us/promo-tracker
>
> ---
>
> Watch a video on how to use the Promotion Tracking Worksheet at www.BirthdayMarketing.us/promo-video

Step 6: Analyze your results

The success or failure of a promotion is measured by how much return you get for your investment (R.O.I). The Promotion Tracking Worksheet will help you keep track of costs, mailing recipients, redemptions, and profits.

The key to making a success of each promotion is to analyze the results of each previous promotion, and see what can be improved at each stage in the Birthday Marketing plan.

For example, if you've getting a weak response from your mailings, you might try making the birthday gift more attractive (i.e. generous), or try a different postcard design that is more attractive or engaging. You can also experiment with mailing to different ZIP codes or neighborhoods.

Or, if the number of people in each birthday dinner group is lower than you want, try changing the conditions for the birthday offer.

Whatever you do, make sure to test only one factor at a time so that if there is an improvement, you can tell what caused the improvement. Also, make sure any results are "statistically significant" before you consider them to be a true improvement.

Statistical significance is a topic too broad to be covered in this short section, but you can find a handy tool for determining the statistical significance of your test results by going to www.SplitTestCalculator.com.

How to Supercharge Your Birthday Marketing

Once you start seeing positive results from doing regular Birthday Marketing postcard mailings, you may want to improve your results and expand your reach to more people.

Adding additional "channels" to your Birthday Marketing can provide the boost you want. Those additional channels can include email, "SMS" or text messages, and online advertising. These channels should be intended to supplement, rather than take the place of, your targeted birthday postcard mailings.

Below are some details on how to implement each of those additional channels to increase your Birthday Marketing results.

Email Birthday Club

Although a postcard mailing campaign can allow you to reach out to people in a specific geographic area with your Birthday Club offer, it does have a few drawbacks.

Postcards cost money to design and print, and postage costs money each time you do a mailing. Design changes to your postcard also cost money. It's difficult to quickly test which postcard design or offer gets the best response rates. And, it takes time and staff to put together a mailing each month if you handle it in-house.

An email-based Birthday Club channel has the advantage of low cost, high share-ability, and decent deliverability. True, you will have to get permission before you email somebody...but once you have their permission, you can send out both annual birthday offers and periodic non-birthday discounts and offers.

Depending on which email service provider you use, an email Birthday Club channel can also have the additional advantage of "set it and forget it" birthday offer messages. These are automatically sent out a set number of days before the person's birthday without you having to schedule them each month. It takes a lot of the time and hassle out of making your email Birthday Club channel work effectively.

Note: not all email service providers offer this "set and forget" birthday message feature. Make sure you choose one that offers this option.

> See which Birthday Club email service provider I recommend by going to www.BirthdayMarketing.us/email-service

With most email service providers, you can also schedule emails to be sent out every month (or whenever you choose), like clockwork.

The only thing left, then, is to get people to sign up for your email Birthday Club channel. This is easily accomplished by having your staff pass out Birthday Club signup forms to all guests, then entering the emails from the completed signup forms into your email service provider.

Most email service providers will also let you import email addresses from a text file, spreadsheet, or database (make sure you check which format they require), as long as you have written permission to email those people.

You'll also want to have a sign-up form on your website for people to opt-in to your email Birthday Club channel when they visit your website.

"SMS" or Text-Message Birthday Club

Even though email is a great way to reach people at low cost, the deliverability (i.e. how many people open your emails) is not as high as it used to be. SPAM filters catch a lot of valid emails, and it's easy to delete an email without ever reading it. That is where SMS, or text messaging, comes in.

Nearly everyone who comes to your restaurant also has a cell phone and the ability to receive text messages. They carry their cell phones with them when they go out to eat. And, best of all, people actually read nearly 100% their text messages, usually within seconds or minutes of receiving them.

What if, the next time these folks dined at your restaurant, they saw a table tent or a banner telling them, "Text BIRTHDAY to 79797 to get a free meal on your birthday"? How many people do you think would sign up right away?

It really is just that easy. Just make sure all of your printed promotional materials tell guests how to sign up for your SMS Birthday Club, and you will start seeing sign-ups.

So, how do you go about sending text messages to these folks? Simple: use an SMS service provider.

An SMS service provider allows you to do many of the same things that an email service provider does, such as accepting sign-ups, maintaining a list of subscribers, and sending out messages.

The main difference between the two service providers is that your text messages will get sent directly to the phones your guests are always carrying with them, instead of their email inboxes. So, your deliverability is super-high, and your response rate is high as well. You can still also send birthday messages every year, as well as regular offers and discounts.

Imagine being able to fill your restaurant on a slow night by sending out a text message to your entire list of SMS Birthday Club subscribers, letting them know about a special you're running that night only. How powerful is that?

The SMS Birthday Club channel is such a powerful tool that it can stand on its own, but it also makes a great complement to your Birthday Marketing targeted postcard mailings.

See which Birthday club SMS service provider I recommend by going to www.BirthdayMarketing.us/sms-provider

---

If you'd prefer a done-for-you SMS Birthday Club, you can find out more about it at www.BirthdayMarketing.us/sms-dfy

Online Birthday Marketing

Email and SMS Birthday Club channels are very powerful ways to increase the effectiveness of your Birthday Marketing efforts. The only problem with them is that they are designed mainly to keep in touch with your existing customers, not to bring in new customers.

What if there were another way to contact new people and invite them to spend their birthday at your restaurant...without the hassle and expense of doing postcard mailings?

Online Birthday Marketing can be the solution you're looking for. With a well-planned online marketing campaign, you can target your ads to people who live near your restaurant. Even better, depending on which advertising platform you use, you can also target your ads to them right before their birthday, while they're making their birthday dinner plans.

If you look at the case studies again, you'll see that both Boneheads Restaurant and Brasilia Churrasco Steakhouse used online marketing to achieve their results.

Both restaurants got a significant number of birthday reservations and guests. Both of them generated significant extra revenue that was directly caused by their online Birthday Marketing. And you can do the same.

One of the great advantages to online Birthday Marketing is that once the marketing system is in place, it makes getting new Birthday Club guests almost hands-free. It is a bit complex getting it set up, but well worth it once it's done.

Even better, you can make it so your online Birthday Marketing system automatically notifies you when a birthday boy or girl signs up to have their birthday meal with you. It's a great way to get instantaneous proof that you're getting results.

And (even more important), you can dramatically increase your results by having your online Birthday Marketing system automatically remind the birthday guest of their reservation date and time so they'll be more likely to come in. This saves you the cost of having your restaurant staff take the time to make follow-up calls to confirm reservations, while still getting incredible results.

Restaurants that we've worked with to set up their online Birthday Marketing channels are getting new Birthday Club reservations every day, like clockwork, without having the expense of buying a list of names & addresses, and the time and effort of printing, addressing, stamping, and mailing postcards. The time savings alone makes online Birthday Marketing a winning method for growing their Birthday Club, and the results speak for themselves.

Of course, if you are getting good results and positive ROI from your targeted Birthday Club postcard mailings, I would continue doing them. Online Birthday Marketing is just a very useful way to amplify your efforts and get incredible, consistent results without a lot of hands-on effort every month.

If you want to skip the time and effort of setting up your own online Birthday Marketing system, we can help. We've developed a proprietary system for targeting thousands of people in your town with your Birthday Club offer in the week leading up to their birthday.

Our system lets these people join your Birthday Club via their smartphone or computer, and then automatically sends you an email or text notification of their birthday meal reservation. We also send them automatic reminders so they're more likely to keep their reservation. It's all very clean and efficient, and saves you a ton of work.

Even better, once they have joined your Birthday Club, you can add them to your Birthday Club email and SMS channels so they get offers by email, as well as another birthday offer right before their next birthday. Your online Birthday Club will continue to grow in size day after day, and year after year, becoming more powerful and effective all the time.

Imagine what a powerful asset it would be to have a Birthday Club list of thousands of local residents who all want to receive regular offers from you, and who look forward each year to celebrating their birthday meal with friends and family at your restaurant. Wouldn't that be an incredible competitive edge to have?

We can help you get the same results with your own online Birthday Marketing channel, using the "secret sauce" of our proprietary system.

Unfortunately, due to the exclusive nature of our online Birthday Marketing system, we can only work with a select number of restaurants in each geographic area. This makes sure that each of the restaurants that we work with gets maximum results on an ongoing basis.

Want to see if your business qualifies for our Done-For-You Online Birthday Marketing System?

Fill out the application form at www.BirthdayMarketing.us/online-club

Summary

We've gone, start to finish, through the process of setting up a successful Birthday Marketing strategy. You understand why it's vital that you build a Birthday Club, and how it can benefit your business. And, now you know how to:

- Increase your short-term and long-term profitability with Birthday Marketing
- Build your customer base and keep them coming back throughout the year
- Plan and execute a successful targeted postcard Birthday Club mailing
- Track your results and see whether your mailings are profitable
- Boost your targeted postcard mailing results using email, SMS / text messaging, and online Birthday Marketing channels

All that's left is to get started building your Birthday Marketing machine and growing your Birthday Club. Make sure to check out the Resources section below for useful templates and tools, how-to videos, recommended service providers, and done-for-you services that can save you time and money.

Also, make sure to re-read the section on Online Birthday Marketing. This is a unique service that we offer to a select few restaurants, which will automate the creation of your Birthday Club and save you tons of time and money.

Resources List

Building Your Targeted Mailing List

- Video: how to build your targeted mailing list

www.BirthdayMarketing.us/build-list

- List broker we recommend

www.BirthdayMarketing.us/list-broker

Postcards & Printed Materials

- Postcards: done-for-you designs

www.BirthdayMarketing.us/postcard-design

- Postcards: printing

www.BirthdayMarketing.us/postcard-printing

- Interior materials: done-for-you designs

www.BirthdayMarketing.us/interior-design

- Interior materials: printing

www.BirthdayMarketing.us/interior-printing

Tracking Your Birthday Marketing Promotions

- Promo Tracking Worksheet: download

www.BirthdayMarketing.us/promo-tracker

- Promo Tracking Worksheet: how-to video

www.BirthdayMarketing.us/promo-video

Email Birthday Club
- Video: setting up an email Birthday Club list
www.BirthdayMarketing.us/email-video
- Email service provider we recommend
www.BirthdayMarketing.us/email-service
- Email Birthday Club: done-for-you service
www.BirthdayMarketing.us/email-dfy

SMS Birthday Club
- SMS service provider we recommend
www.BirthdayMarketing.us/sms-provider
- Interior materials: printing
www.BirthdayMarketing.us/sms-printing

Done-For-You Birthday Marketing Services
- Done-for-you postcard Birthday Marketing
www.BirthdayMarketing.us/postcard-dfy
- Done-for-you email Birthday Club
www.BirthdayMarketing.us/email-dfy
- Done-for-you SMS Birthday Club
www.BirthdayMarketing.us/sms-dfy

<u>Online Birthday Club Services</u>

- **Done-for-you online Birthday Marketing**
  www.BirthdayMarketing.us/online-club